First Facts

MEERKATS, MOLES, AND VOLES
ANIMALS OF THE UNDERGROUND

by Jody Sullivan Rake

Consultant:
Shala Hankison, PhD
Assistant Professor, Department of Zoology
Ohio Wesleyan University
Deleware, Ohio

CAPSTONE PRESS
a capstone imprint

First Facts are published by Capstone Press,
1710 Roe Crest Drive, North Mankato, Minnesota 56003
www.capstonepub.com

Library of Congress Cataloging-in-Publication Data
Rake, Jody Sullivan, author.
  Meerkats, moles, and voles animals of the underground / by Jody Sullivan Rake.
    pages cm. — (First facts. Underground safari)
  Summary: "Teaches readers about various vertebrate animals that burrow underground"—Provided by publisher.
  Includes bibliographical references and index.
  ISBN 978-1-4914-5060-4 (library binding)
  ISBN 978-1-4914-5090-1 (eBook PDF)
1. Burrowing animals—Juvenile literature. 2. Burrowing animals—Habitations—Juvenle literature. 3. Underground ecology—Juvenile literature. I. Title.
  QL756.15.R35 2016
  591.56'48—dc23
                        2014047458

Editorial Credits
Abby Colich, editor; Heidi Thompson, designer; Jo Miller, media researcher; Katy LaVigne, production specialist

Photo Credits
Dreamstime: Aughty Venable, 11, Michael Elliot, 9, Vaulot, 19; Glow Images/Arco Images RM/Layer, W., 7; Newscom: imageBROKER/Marko König, 5, Minden Pictures/FLPA/Dembinsky Photo Ass., 13, Photoshot/NHPA/Chris Mattison, 21, Photoshot/NHPA/Karl Switak, 20, Photoshot/NHPA/Manfred Danegger, 15; Shutterstock: David Nagy, 17, Grimplet, cover (middle), ivandon, cover (right), KRUKAO cover (background), 1, Martin Lehmann, 8, nattanan726, cover (left), 14, WOLF AVNI, 2-3

Design Elements
Shutterstock: Hal_P, LudmilaM

Printed in China by Nordica
0415/CA21500544
042015   008845NORDF15

ground squirrels

TABLE OF CONTENTS

A HIDDEN WORLD

Thousands of animals live in the ground below your feet. These animals dig homes called *burrows*. A burrow protects animals from bad weather and *predators*.

Burrows can be small holes or long tunnels. Some burrows are like huge, winding underground cities. Most burrows have areas like rooms in a house. There are places to sleep, store food, and get rid of body waste.

burrow—a tunnel or hole in the ground made or used by an animal

predator—an animal that hunts other animals for food

▲ Mongolian gerbil

RODENTS ALL AROUND

Many burrowing animals are *rodents*.
Rodents include mice, rats, and squirrels.

Gophers are small rodents that dig
tunnels all day. They eat the roots of grass
and other plants. Gophers have pouches
in their cheeks. They carry food to their
burrows in the pouches.

Voles are tiny mouselike rodents.
They are sometimes called field mice.
Voles eat roots and bulbs underground.

rodent—a mammal with long front teeth used for gnawing

DIG IN!

A female vole can have up to 100 babies a year.

▼ **bank vole with babies**

SQUIRRELS AND THEIR COUSINS

You've probably seen squirrels playing in trees. But did you know some squirrels live underground? Underground squirrels eat plants and seeds. A cousin of the squirrel, the chipmunk, burrows underground too.

Prairie dogs are a type of squirrel. Below prairies they dig large burrows called towns. Groundhogs are also called woodchucks. These animals stuff themselves with food in the fall. Then they *hibernate* underground all winter.

groundhog

prairie—a large area of flat or rolling grassland with few or no trees

hibernate—to spend winter in a deep sleep

▲ prairie dogs

The largest prairie dog town ever measured was 25,000 square miles (65,000 square kilometers). That's about the size of West Virginia! It was home to about 400 million prairie dogs!

MORE UNDERGROUND FAMILIES

Naked mole-rats are neither moles nor rats. These hairless rodents spend their entire lives burrowing in a *colony*. One colony may be as large as six football fields.

Rabbits are built for hopping above ground. But they live in underground homes. Rabbits build burrow towns called *warrens*. About 20 rabbits live in a warren.

colony—a group of the same kind of animal

warren—a network of underground tunnels built by rabbits for safety and sleeping

▼ naked mole-rat

11

TINY TUNNELERS

Moles and shrews spend almost all their lives underground. Both of these animals are blind. Their smell and touch senses are very strong. These abilities help them get around.

The star-nosed mole has 22 *tentacles* around its nose. The tentacles are full of tiny *sensors*. They sense the size, shape, and movement things underground.

DIG IN!

Moles are small, but shrews are even smaller. An adult Etruscan shrew can fit in a teaspoon!

tentacle—a long, armlike body part some animals use to touch, grab, or smell
sensor—a body part that sends messages to the brain

star-nosed mole

MEAT-EATING EARTH MOVERS

Many meat eaters are burrowers.
Meerkats take over burrows dug by other
animals. A group of 20 to 30 meerkats may
live in a burrow. Meerkats eat bugs, birds,
and lizards.

The biggest burrowers of
all are bears. Bears do not
hibernate the same way
other animals do. But
bears do spend all
winter in underground
dens. They move less
and lose weight in the
colder months.

▶ meerkats

DIG IN!

Burrowers are needed in nature. When they move soil around, it helps plants grow.

▲ **European brown bear**

15

NOT ALL BIRDS LIVE IN TREES

The burrowing owl prefers a worm's eye view of the world. These owls live in open treeless areas in North and South America. They take shelter in burrows dug by prairie dogs.

You won't find the Magellanic penguin on ice. This penguin lives in the warm *tropics*. It escapes the heat by sliding into burrows.

DIG IN!

Burrowing owls collect **mammal** poop to put around their nests. This waste attracts dung beetles, one of their favorite foods.

tropics—a warm region of Earth that is near the equator

mammal—a warm-blooded animal that breathes air, has hair or fur, and feeds milk to its young

burrowing owl

UNDERWATER BURROWS

For some fish the bottom of the ocean is not deep enough. Gobies and jawfish dig out sand with their mouths. Then they burrow into the seafloor.

The desert pupfish is used to life without much water. This fish can survive in only 0.5 inch (1.3 centimeters) of water! If water gets even lower, the fish burrows in the mud.

The desert pupfish is one of the most *endangered* animals in the world.

DIG IN!

endangered—in danger of dying out

18

goby ◄

19

COLD-BLOODED CAVERS

Many *cold-blooded* creatures live in burrows. To escape the heat, the desert tortoise spends close to 23 hours a day in a burrow.

Frogs, toads, and salamanders need to stay wet to survive. If their water hole dries up, they burrow into the mud to stay damp.

California desert tortoise ▶

cold-blooded—having a body temperature that changes with the surrounding temperature

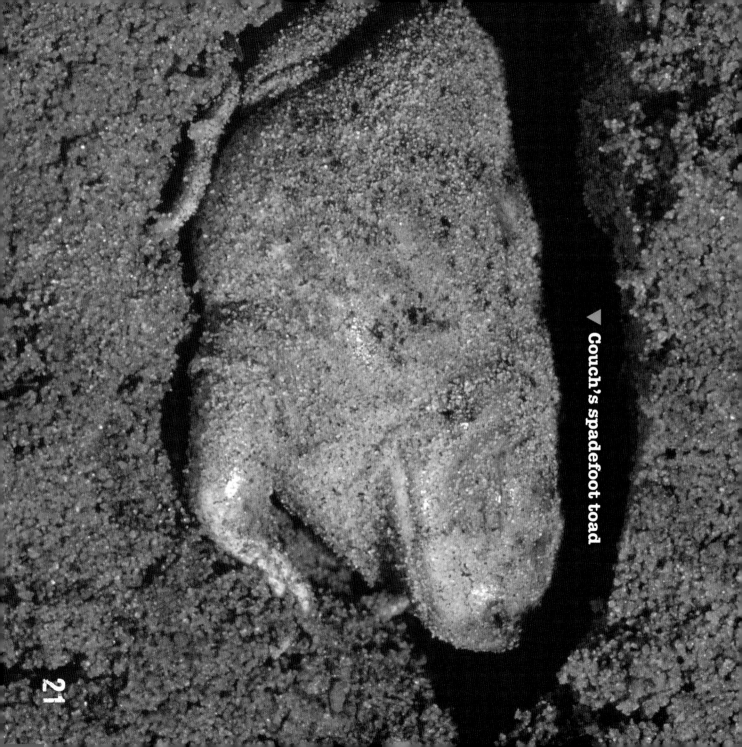

▼ Couch's spadefoot toad

GLOSSARY

burrow (BUHR-oh)—a tunnel or hole in the ground made or used by an animal

cold-blooded (KOHLD-BLUHD-id)—having a body temperature that changes with the surrounding temperature

colony (KAH-luh-nee)—a group of the same kind of animal

endangered (in-DAYN-juhrd)—in danger of dying out

hibernate (HYE-bur-nate)—to spend winter in a deep sleep

mammal (MAM-uhl)—a warm-blooded animal that breathes air, has hair or fur, and feeds milk to its young

prairie (PRAIR-ee)—a large area of flat or rolling grassland with few or no trees

predator (PRED-uh-tur)—an animal that hunts other animals for food

rodent (ROHD-uhnt)—a mammal with long front teeth used for gnawing

sensor (SEN-sur)—a body part that sends messages to the brain

tentacle (TEN-tuh-kuhl)—a long, armlike body part some animals use to touch, grab, or smell

tropics (TROP-iks)—a warm region of Earth that is near the equator

warren (WOR-uhn)—a network of underground tunnels built by rabbits for safety and sleeping

READ MORE

Phillips, Dee. *Groundhog's Burrow. The Hole Truth!: Underground Animal Life.* New York: Bearport Publishing, 2012.

Racanelli, Marie. *Underground Animals. Crazy Nature.* New York: PowerKids Press, 2010.

Sebastian, Emily. *Moles. Animals Underground.* New York: Rosen/PowerKids Press, 2012.

INTERNET SITES

FactHound offers a safe, fun way to find Internet sites related to this book. All of the sites on FactHound have been researched by our staff.

Here's all you do:

Visit *www.facthound.com*

Type in this code: 9781491450604

Check out projects, games and lots more at
www.capstonekids.com

CRITICAL THINKING USING THE COMMON CORE

1. List three reasons animals live underground. (Key Ideas and Details)

2. Reread page 12. Why might some animals that live underground not need to see? Are they at a disadvantage compared to burrowers that can see? Support your answer. (Integration of Knowledge and Ideas)

3. Reread pages 14 and 16. Why do you think a bear spends winter in a den? How is this different from the reason that the Magellanic penguin burrows? (Craft and Structure)

INDEX